FEELINGS

2022

WOODROW WALLACE

To order additional copies of this book, contact:
Xlibris
844-714-8691
www.Xlibris.com
Orders@Xlibris.com

ISBN: Softcover   978-1-6698-4694-9
        Hardcover   978-1-6698-4711-3
        EBook   978-1-6698-4695-6

Print information available on the last page

Rev. date: 09/15/2022

CONTENTS

Post covid-19???Hmmm....... (UKRAINE)

Crimea 2022
It happened, The-Mad-MAN did it. Putin's
Russia Changed the world. Its May 17,
2022 and 10 people were gunned down in
Buffalo, New York...In a supermarket...

"DEPRESSION"

THE AWAKENED MAN, SLEEP-WALKS
THROUGH THE NIGHTED DAY;
WITH AN URGENCY OF SLOTH
BEAMING THE PERFECT DULLNESS;
With A HEART GONE JARVIS
SMILING HIS SALTY TEARS;
WITH JAYOUS SADNESS
EXPOSING DECADES,
WITH AN EYE-FLASH;
ONLY SHOUTING IN SILENCE
FOR ANOTHER LIFE TO DO OVER.

ITS A STRANGE TIME OF THE YEAR IN
ASTRONOMICAL TERMS.

COVID-19 ROCKED OUR WORLD. BELIEVE
ME "WE ONLY HAVE ONE"......... CLIMATE
CHANGE IS BACK UP TO BE RECKONED
WITH AGAIN...

"FOOL'S GOLD"

I PITY THE MAN,
WHO FINDS FOOL'S GOLD;
FOOL'S GOLD HURTS SO BAD,
IT CAN MAKE YOU CRY;
SOMETIMES YOU REMINIISCE,
HOW FOOL'S GOLD USE TO BE;

SOMETIMES YOU SIT BACK,
AND SMELL, OLD FOOL'S GOLD;
SOMETIMES IN YOUR HEAD,
YOU TALK TO THE MEMORIES,
OF FOOL'S GOLD
SOMETIMES, YOU HATE YOURSELF,
FOR FINDING FOOL'S GOLD;
SOME PEOPLE. NEVER FIND FOOL'S GOLD
THAT CAN BE WORSE THAN THE GOLD;
THIS I DO KNOW!
WHEN YOU LOSE, FOOL'S GOLD,
AND IT DRAWS TO AN END-
THAT'S WHEN THE REAL PAIN BEGIN!
SO, I HATE YOU, FOOL'S GOLD,
DON'T EVER FALL ON ME AGAIN-
YOU HURT SO DAMNED GOOD,
BUT, YOU'RE TRULY, NOT MY FRIEND.

WE STILL HAVE NOT DEALT WITH THE
GUNS IN OUR SOCIETY. ITS LIKE RACISM,
WE ARE SCARED OF THE TRUTH! NOT AFRAID.

SCARED! SCARED!

I REPEAT! IT SEEMED SO LONG AGO......
YET HERE WE ARE AGAIN-BUT IS IT NOT
2022?

"CAPITOL HEIGHTS-2015"

I STEPPED OUTSIDE, THE OTHER DAY
AND RATA-TATA-TAT-TAT TAT
ANOTHER BLACK BROTHER
LYING ON HIS BACK.

THIS IS WHAT WE DO
TO EACH OTHER-
A COWARDLY–ASS-ACT
DONE UNDER COVER.

ALL I KNOW IS,
I'M FULL OF SORROW-
BECAUSE, I GOT TO WALK
THAT PARKING LOT, TOMORROW.

BUT WE CALL THIS SHIT
BEING A MAN;
REALLY, WE'RE ACTING OUT
THE OVERSEER'S PLAN.

YEAH, POP-POP-POP-POP-POP
WE DON'T GIVE-A-DAM-
WE MAKE SURE THE NEW WOLRD ORDER
GETS ITS GREEN EGGS AND HAM.

SO, BLACKS AND WHITES, GOT TOGETHER
MAN THAT SHIT WAS TRULY CLEVER;
GEORGE FLOYD LEFT US CRYING
BUFFALO 2022,
BLACK PEOPLE ARE STILL DYING.

I KNOW THIS SHIT SOUNDS REAL HARSH
BUT, I DON'T WANT TO SEE YOU DIE
IN REALITY, SAD MOVIES MAKE ME CRY.

CALL ME NAMES, OR WHAT YOU WILL-
SOME ILLITERATE PEOPLE, JUST KILL;
GO TO PRISON AND SAY, I'M NO PUNK
FACT IS, YOU'RE A REAL, FREAKING GUMP.

NOW, I HAVE YOUR ATTENTION
WE CAN STOP PAYING, JIMMY LYNCH'S PENSION;

THERE ARE BETTER WAYS
TO COMMINICATE
SHOW SOME LOVE, STOP THE HATE.

KILLING MY BROTHER, DIMINISHES ME
BUT, I GUESS, UNTIL WE CAN SEE;
NO MAN IS AN ISLAND,
JUST A BRANCH ON THE TREE.

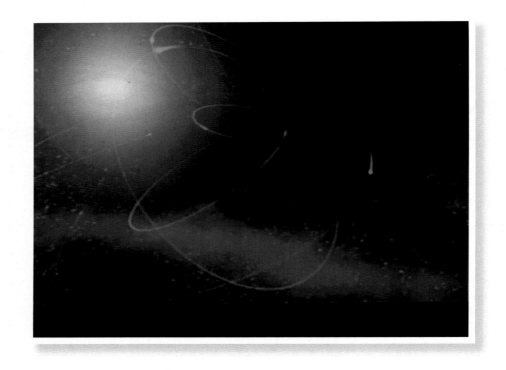

WHERE IS UKRAINE AND RUSSIA? ITS JULY 2022........

"AN OBSERVATION"

All hell has broken loose, on this planet
We war with each other, and take it for granted;
All hell has broken lose, on this stellar rock
The only thing consistent, is the ticking clock.

All hell has broken lose, on this rotating ball
Don't point the finger, include us all;
All hell has broken lose, on this floating satellite
It's a perpetual struggle, day and night.

All hell has broken lose, on three from the sun
face the facts, there is nowhere to run;
All hell has broken lose, on this spinning sphere
And not one, gives-a-dam, or shed a tear.

All hell has broken lose, on this 4-season resort
And the powers to be, are not about to abort;

All hell has broken lose, on this Human Lot
Ozone is weakening, while cold places get hot.
All hell has broken lose, on God's green earth
We are killing each other, over concrete turf;
All hell has broken lose, on Adam's paradise
Everyone wants to give, some kind of advice.

"AN OBSERVATION"

All hell has broken lose, on this solar band
The 4-Horsemen are riding, throughout the land;
All hell has broken lose, on this drifting tomb
And we are killing each other, even in the womb.

All hell has broken lose, on our only home
And all the damage done, is our own;
All hell has broken lose, on this 7-11
Where is the King? Where is Heaven?

"TRANSPARENCY"

(You want)
So, you want to be President Of these United States-
But you too damned shaky To set that date.

So, you want to be CEO
Of a corporate IBM
But, you want step out
On that damned limb.

So, you want to be rich
And live the good-ole life- But, you too damned
weak To give up, your vice.

So, you want to be shot caller In your entire life-
But, you want the mistress And keep the loving
wife.

So, you want to see justice Equality, and fair play-
But, you're too damned blind To see the truth,
today.

"A DEATH-ROW DREAM"

Man! Man! Man!
How the Hell, I get here? Dam! Dam! Dam!
And the end, keeps drawing near.

"STUCK IN THE HOOD"

So, you think you're a bad-ass Because your pants hang down- Could you really be saying? This is my hand-me-down.

So, you think you're a cool-mother Because you smoke cigarettes- Could you really be saying? You will have many regrets.

So, you think you are top-dog Because you drink and use dope- Could you really be saying? You have little or no hope.

So, you knocked your girl up Then fled the scene- Could you really be saying? I've created another, Ghetto Queen.

So, you think you're the man So it seems- Could you really be saying? I'm drowning in systemic dreams.

"HEY YOU-REALLY"

Please, hear these words
You print really good,
in your books
You sing really good,
on your records
You testify really good,
to the interviewer
You pray really good,
to your God
You advise really good,
on the camera
You speak really good,
to heads of states
---However---
When I look out my window When I walk out my
door
I do not see you
---Because--- You do not come to help me

You do not bring inspiration daily
You come when
you want my vote
---And---
You use me in your speeches
You use me in your rhetoric
You use me in your political maundering!
---By the way---
If this offend, or put you, on the defense
Perhaps, you need to re-examine, your actions
pretend, you really, have no idea,
what this means
Because, you're really
The killer, of my dreams.

"I WITNESS"

Remember, I saw you
I saw you, steal from us
I saw you, hold us hostage
I saw you, kill the great leaders
I saw you, deceive my Fore-Fathers
I saw you, promise the lie
I saw you,
War with the world
I saw you,
Distribute death! Remember, I saw you

"THE TOUGH BOYS AND GIRLS"

"You Want To Know How Tough I AM?"

From the past to the future, and all between
I'm the toughest, poet, you ever seen;
I'm SUPER MOUTH
Straight out of the Mid-Freaking-South.
I've had more hard times, than an average man
I got the coldest mouth, in the entire land;
Over in China, they call me, Dr. Talk
I'm slapping losers around, and walking the walk.
I went to the North Pole, just to spit on the moon
I walked through the Himalayas, naked, like Daniel Boone.
I went to Africa, to have a little fun
I went deep in the jungle, without a loaded gun;
Slapped a gorilla, upside the head
Said, flinch big guy, and you dead.
I smoked a two-gallon bong, with King Kong
And made Kong bust, his big-ass lungs.
I'll snap on your body, like a gator
Leave you looking, like mash potato.
I got no guidelines, or dog-gone rules

I'll make a son-of-a-gun sing the blues;
And you better not squeal, or freaking hollow
Because I'll whip on your butt, again tomorrow.

I'm worse, than a seven-year itch
I'll turn you out, like a $2.00 witch;
I wear suites, straight from my tailors
I smash losers up, like tractor trailers.

You want to know; how tough I am?
Just ask, your well known, Uncle Sam.
I joined the arm-forces, to blow up shit
Two days in, they begged me, to quit;
I told my Drill Sargent he was a jackass
Shut-up, and give me the dam class.

I told my Company Commander,
Don't make no noise
Or I'll whip your ass, like Chuck Norris;
From basic training, to the CIA
I gave them Folks, a bad-ass-day.

You want to know; how tough I can be?
Listen to these rhymes, and you will see.

I high-jacked an aircraft carrier, on my first night
I told the President, I'm ready to freaking fight;
I yelled to the crew, stand fast, and you
better not run
Or you answer, to Super Mouth's freaking gun.
The crew yelled back, we with you, all the dam way
Just give the order, we'll blow some shit up today;
I blew off, about six nukes, just for fun
And returned to America, on the run.

When my two feet, hit dry land
I went straight to the casino, the bankrupt Grand;
I bet a counterfeit thousand, on the field
Those puppies threw 12, and sealed the deal.
I told the pit boss, to let it ride again
He said screw you, you ain't my, long lost friend;
I grabbed my winnings and put it in the wind
Went out on the town, with my lady friends.

"SUPER MOUTH'S POETRY AT FORT DIX PRISON"

I'm gonna tell you, right from the start
What you about to hear, ain't for the faint of heart;
If you sensitive, like a weak old Joe
Cover your ears or hit the front door.
My name is Super Mouth, I carry gats
I run up the bad guys murder stats;
I got a base of Poets, and crowd of fans
I got Poets working, over in Afghanistan
Just for sport, I Huck up the Klu Klux Klan
I got thousands of poems, on these hands.
Truth be known, this is fact
I stirred up some trouble, over in Iraq;
When I heard, Ben Laden, had dropped those towers
I said, this pigga, done messed up my New York
Poets working hours.

It ain't all about Obama, and his crew
I avenged those towers and some Taliban too.
I'm a cold Poet, can't you see?
Straight out of Memphis, by way of D.C.
Poetry is alive, and also well
A temporary set-back, when a lie prevails.
Lies are so mean, vicious, and slick
It'll make a Poet, want to quit;
Poetry wrapped up and began to leave
Lie jumps up, and grab Poetry's by the sleeve;
And this is what, the lie said:
Super, I'll break your will and bash that head,
Super replied, no thanks lie, Freddie is dead.
The lie yelled, before I give up my rein, I'll set in gasoline
Super smirked, I'll lite it, and burn you like a dope, Feign.
Lie looked at Super, with a big head frown
Asked, what you want, since you done got down?

Super said, park me a limo, on this pound;
I'm gonna need a ride to the next dam town
On that day, don't wear no doctor's gown;
And tell your boss, I ain't fucking around.
The lie looked disheveled and out of place
Super said, get back in your hole and clean up
your face.
The lie stepped back, and asked, is all that mean
talk necessary?
Super replied, you'll find out, if ain't no paper on
my commissary.
The lie looked up at Super, with tears in its eyes
Super said, lie, this ain't my last good-byes.
I'm a thorough Poet, with the heart of a lion
Every time I turn a lie out, I leave it crying;
You see, can't no weak lie, role with me
I'm slapping lies around, like Bruce Lee;
This poetry goes back, to Tim-Buck-Tu
This is my job, this is what a Poet do.

I'm a dog-gone big-baler
Word on the pound,
I'm the number 1 shot caller;
When I get hungry, I send piggas, straight to the kitchen
They can't come back, with less than 20 pieces of chicken.
If they get caught, I kick-em in the ass, and break their neck
That's how a Poet, in Dix, get respect;
I'm an old time Poet, and I play my part
I told you, this Poetry, ain't for the faint of heart.
You want to know, what a Poet do-when on the street?
Well, pull up a chair, let me give you a knee knocking treat.
I got Poets working out of China, and V[ET Nam
I feed em' peanut butter, and egg Foo Yong;
At the age of 9, I turned my first Poet out
On Government cheese and sauerkraut.

I make a Poet recite, loud like a pig
Listen, they'll blow back your wig.
I'm gonna find me, a super-head momma
Recite my Poetry, all this summer;
My nickname, is Doctor-Dunk-A-hick
I write rhymes, with Taylor Made golf sticks
I'm walking tall, with a woman size chick.
I got a dog down South, name 'POE Rick'.

POE RICK

//
Now, up North, I got a mean Chicago crew
My Poets work 24-7, including holidays too;
My Poets dress out, in micro-minies

With fish-net panties, and nylon skinnies.
Wearing Beyoncé bras, pushing McLaren cars
I got them Poets, looking like super stars;
My Poets, work up and down Halstead street
All my Poets, got quota to meet.
Winter-time, that Chicago hawk is blowing
But this knot in our pockets, just keep on growing;
My Chicago Poets, work straight through the winter
They eat fish-head soup, and alligator for dinner.
On Sunday evenings during family hour
My Poets slanging rhymes, out of Chrysler Tower;
When I'm in Chicago, and things ain't nice
I go to Al Capone's grave, and ask for advice.
///
In New York, I got a bad ass French Creole crew, called Sweet Satin
You can buy stock, in this crew, down in Manhattan.
In the Big Apple, I hang out with bank like Andy Bean

We trading rhymes and lines, out of Jamaica Queens;
I got all my crews wearing Maybeline.
I got a full-time crew, working out of Harlem too
And over 300 Poets, slanging out the zoo;
I got a thorough, uptown, New York crew
Thinking, about hiring Merle Lynch, as my stock broker too;
Because I'm bullish, on my New York crew.
Da Ha, Da Ha, Da Ha, I'm the big Duke
Working these crews, like Cool Hand Luke.
///
Now, down in Memphis, on 3rd and Beale
I got my crews, hitting them tills;
From Main Street, to Handy Park
Working them crews, day through dark.
I'm working these crews, the hard way
Working these crews, on Labor Day.
I got them crews, riding on mopeds
Spreading that knowledge, before its dead;
I got them crews, working those strips

Getting that paper, and doing monkey flips.
My crews out there, educating them hicks
Weaving and bobbing, all on them tricks;
My crews, working out the New Daisy
Reciting that word, like they're crazy;
And what you heard, ain't no rumors
I got Grannies reciting in wartime bloomers.
//
Now, on the streets, back in D.C.
I'm hanging out, in celebrity bars
Working crews, out of sports cars;
Conversing with politicians, and movie stars
Singing hooks, with Bruno Mars.
When all my crews, come to town
We got front row seats, watching Chris Brown;
I got Little Wayne, checking our bags
I'm slapping Nicki Minaj, on her big fat ---.
Want to know, what else I do
Michelle Obama, run my D.C. crew
With Nancy Pelosi, moon-lighting too.

I ain't playing around, I'm having a fit
Poetry ain't dead, these crews wanna quit;
So, listen up, my good friend
This poetic rhyming, will never end;
I got a couple of things, you need to know
Like Captain Picard, I'm gonna make it so.
From Memphis, Chicago, New York, to D.C.
You better keep your crews, away from me;
One last thing, before I leave this rock
My time has wound down, on this clock.
I'm gonna give these CO's, a freaking fit
Because I'm done, with this, dog-gone-bit;
The heck with Big Brother's old crew
With these few days, I got left to do
You can find me chill-in, down in 5702;
And you best believe, this is fact
Like Swartz-A-Pigga, this Poetry is back!

"SUPER MOUTH REMINISCING"

I remember back in `72, I didn't give-a-fuck
I'd pull up, on the poetry track, in a dump
truck;
With 34 Poets, riding in the back
Like they were in a Candy-Coated-Cadillac.

I'd pull that leaver, and the bed drop down
Planting, all my Poets, firmly on the ground;
Wearing guarder belts, and 3 inch heels
Ready to rhyme, with looks to kill;
Looking fresh, and smelling good
Like a crew of Poets, straight from the hood.
My bottom Poet, would give the speech
Man, that Poet, could really preach;
She told them fine little`Souls
Slang that Poetry, like its gold.
Remember, when you hit them doors
You reciting from Super Mouth's, stores;
So, stand up straight, and walk with class
Because you're the best, that Poetry has.

"SUPER MOUTH MEETS 2 ROGUE COPS"

2022, on April Fool's Day
Two rogue cops, tried to block my way
This is what, those rogues, had to say;
Super, we need to see your ID
I said, rogues, stop messing with me.

They said, Dog, either comply, or go to jail
I replied, 'and you rogues are going to hell;
I don't give-a-huck about the law
I'll make you eat hot dogs and cold slaw.'

Johnny Law, you need to, let me through
Because a brawl is what's coming to you;
They replied, you must be, Super Mouth
Yah, straight from the Mid-Freaking-South.

Super, we are the dog-gone law
Super, left hooked that rogue, in his jaw.
People on the sidewalk, started to grin

Super, upper-cupped his partner, in his chin.
And yelled, Law-Dog, I don't play
I got serious stuff, to do today;
First cop, yelled, and reached for his iron
Super hit him so hard, he started crying.
They finally caught Super, out in L.A.
Believe me, it didn't go their way;
They took Super before the judge, in his best dress-
Judge said, don't come in here, with that foolish mess.
Super said, Judge, to be honest, I got to roam
Because I got crews, I need to check on;
Judge said, 50 years is what you face Super said, pardon me judge, you looking at the wrong case.
Another thing, I ain't guilty, of put on that fit
Because them rogues, could have been done quit;
Judge said, screw you, what you want me to do?
Super said, send me back, to my East Coast crew;
Before I split your head, to the freaking fat

With Babe Ruth's, baseball bat.
Judge said, Super! what you trying to say?
Super said, if you don't let me leave L.A.
This is gonna be, your worse freaking day.

Judge said, Super, I order you out of this town
Super said, okay your honor, I'm East bound;
And you can pick up your crew, just outside of town.
Super left there, with his back to the wind
Headed East, to spit that, Poetry again.

"JUICY JOY"

She's juicy Joy, from Ilinoy, and a feign
She Turn more tricks, than a, Ringling Brother's team;
Her reach is deeper, than the Atlantic Ocean

She is deadlier, than a poison potion.
She's had more-hard times, than Pleasing Pam
She's more popular than weed,
Over in Amsterdam;
Up in Canada, she's like Wonder Woman
She mail her word, with a court summon.

Down in South America, she go big and tall
Speaking her word, through collect call.

She lectured twenty days, and twenty nights
Her face lit up, like the Northern lights;
She kissed a blind man, and gave him sight
The blind man's wife, said, "that shit ain't right!"
She played Tiger Woods, and made him fist pump
She stuffed Hulk Hogan, in a closed trunk;
She made Big foot, scream out loud
All her stakeholders, felt real proud.

She sometimes work, with 'Ole Saint Nick
Because she is, Madam Super Trick;
She finally found, the Himalayan Yeti
Made him look like cooked spaghetti.

Now, call her a lie, Mr. Bama
She'll pound you with that sludge-hammer;
She's like an aging liquor, setting on a shelf
She'll make you, second guess yourself.

She's like a good meal, but she ain't cheap
she'll have your man, talking in his sleep;
And this ain't, no made-up-ploy
Listen long enough, he'll scream, Juicy Joy.

Her hug is so sweet, firm, and tight
She broke Jesse Owens record, late, last night;
Listen to her voice, when she talk
Made James Brown, do his camel walk.

She got the best loving, in the entire land
She makes her lover scream, like Tarzan;
She hypnotized a gorilla, with a stick
Made him work, until he got sick.
She fought a grizzly bear, until he passed out
Woke the beast, and stumped on his snout;

She drank a cold glass of water
And made that grizzly, fight even harder.

Listen, she is chief lover, in this world
She's a full-grown woman, not a girl;
See those beautiful little hands
She'll slap the sense, out your man.
Serving it up fresh, from me to you
Turning Grey skies, into blue;
So back the heck up, Baby Boo This is Juicy Joy's,
poetic, Crew.

//

"TAY TAY MEETS FACE"

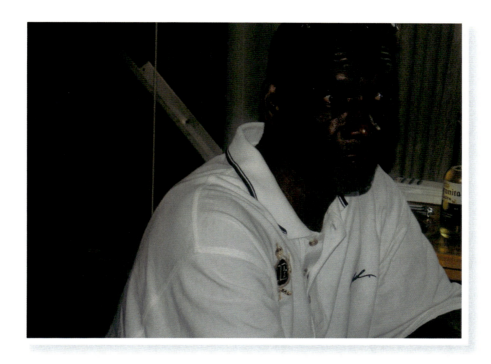

It was dusk dark, on his 40th birthday
Something caught the eye, of Tay Tay;
He looked out his window, and what did he see?
A mean scary face, looking back at he;
He asked, what the Huck, are you doing out there?

The face answered, bring your son-so out here.
Tay Tay replied, I ain't scared, and that's a fact
Face bellowed, I can't tell, with all that yack;
Listen, my name is Tay Tay, Cousin to Ray Ray
I'm bundling misfits, like a bale of hay.
So, don't write a check, you can't cash
Face replied, I'll smoke you, and make my dash;
Tay Tay said, before you cross that deadly street
I'm gonna James Brown on you, with my
With my hands and my feet
Mess around Tay Tay, and miss a step
Face gonna have you, begging for help;
You talk real fast Face, and sort of mean
I'll stitch you up, like a sowing machine.
Dam you Tay Tay, I want be had
I'm gonna whip you, like I'm your Dad;
And your momma, gonna scream loud too
Because you will turn, from black to blue.
Face, I'm gonna turn you out, like a fresh score
As soon, as I step out, this dog-gone door;

Yah Tay Tay, your tongue may move, your eyes may see
But you gonna catch, a whole-lotta-hell, tussling with me.
Tay Tay jumped out that door, like a lightning bolt
Grabbed face by his freaking throat;
Slammed him up against a utility pole
And planted his boot, deep in his soul.
Face managed to struggle, and wiggle free
Busted Tay Tay's nose, with a Christmas tree;
Tay Tay yelled, dog, you done, messed up
Side-stepped Face, and caught him, with an upper cup.
Face slid, about a half-a-block
His tongue fell out, like a coo coo clock;
Now, many a story have been told
But this is true, so-help-my soul.
Face never woke up, from that excursion
And I swear by, this hilarious version.

"RUBY RED CONFRONTS GOOD PLEASING PAM"

Early, one Saturday morning, at Ole-Cafe
Ruby Red was about, to start her day;
When Birdman, swooped in with a smile
And dropped some gossip, a lot of jive.
He said, Ruby Red, a woman up the way
Is loving your man, night and day;
Ruby asked, who is she, where does she reside?
Up the hill, and about, a country mile.
She's known, as Good Pleasing Pam
Truth be known, she don't give a dam;
One more thing, you need to know
She keeps coming for more and more.
Ruby Red, jumped up, like a mad dog
Slobbing at the mouth, grunting like a hog;
Out the door, and up the hill
Pushing that Cadillac, ready to kill.
She arrived at 44 North West
Good Pleasing Pam's, place of rest;

A bang on the door, and a ring of the bell
Backed up, with a vicious dam yell.
The door opens, and up pops Pam
Ruby yelled, God dam! You must be Pam!
Yes I am, better known, as Good Pleasing Pam!
I'm six four, and a mean ass whore,
What the hell, you doing, banging on my door?
My name is Ruby Red, Where's my man, Freaky Fred?
I heard he been sleeping, in your bed,
And some say, you been giving him head.
Woman are you crazy, or just absurd?
You been listening, to that damned Bird?
You best be getting, on your freaking way
Before I send you busted-up,
Back to Ole Cafe.
Ruby replied, dam you Pam,
I'll chop you up, like a ham
Give you a whipping for sure
To last your ass, forever more.
Pam yelled, hold it witch, you better take a rest

Before I drop-kick you, in your chest;
Ruby Red, reached for the freaking door
Good Pleasing Pam, slugged that whore.
Knocked Ruby Red, flat on her back
And body slammed her, on her Cadillac
Ruby Red stood up, and let out a moan
Judo kicked Pam, upside her big dam dome.
Good Pleasing Pam, Pulled up a mail box
Stalked Ruby Red, like a cunning fox;
Pam hit Ruby, so freaking hard
Ruby let out, an earth quaking fart.
Fell to her knees, and looked to the sky
And screamed, bitch! Prepare to die;
Ruby gave Good Pleasing Pam, a snap-mare
Knocked all the wind, out that big bear.
Pam elbowed Ruby, in her throat
Had her gagging, like a billy goat;
Followed up, with a mean neck-breaker
Laid Ruby out, for the undertaker.
Pam threw Ruby into her Cadillac
Told Ruby, don't ever come back!

Ruby Red left there, with nothing to say
Making her way back, to ole Cafe.
Birdman started laughing, and cutting a jig
Look like somebody, messed up your wig;
Your head been cut, to the freaking fat
Look like you ran into, a real dirty rat.
I told ya' ll, this heifer, is just a lot of talk
I'm the only Big Guy, walking the walk;
Look at you, face all bloody, black, and blue
Good Pleasing Pam, done hucked all over you.
Ruby Red Hit Birdman so hard, he lost his breathe
When he woke up, he had defecated on himself;
Ruby Red picked Birdman up, by his tongue
Bounced him across the table, like ping pong.
Birdman yelled, Ruby please, have mercy on me!
Ruby kicked him in butt, all the way up to her knee;
Dragged him outside, and tied him to a tree
I want all you buzzards, gather around and see;
This son-of-a-gun, gonna stop messing with me.
Birdman looked up to the sky,

And began to cry;
He pleaded, If anyone, care about poor little me
Please give me a reprieve, and set me free.
Suddenly, a hummer, came roaring down the street
A brawd stepped out, with two big feet;
None other, then Good Pleasing Pam
Birdman yelled, please help me Mam!
Pam asked Birdman, What's the ruckus out here?
Birdman replied, I was just having a beer
Now, Ruby, got me, in great freaking fear,
Please............ help me Cuss,
I was just telling her, how much a lady you wuss.
Good Pleasing Pam, began to preach
I got another lesson for you, I must teach;
Pam grabbed Ruby, by her big long nose
Started to whip on her, with a water hose.

Ruby monkey flipped Pam, to the side walk
And said, I'm sick of your, witch-ass-talk;
Pam jumped up, charged Ruby, with her head down

Ruby bull-dogged Pam big butt, to the ground.
Pam rolled over and sprung to her feet
knee flipped Ruby, into an army jeep;
Meanwhile, Birdman, had wiggled free
And asked, Ruby Red, what's it gonna be?
Cause Good Pleasing Pam, gonna avenge me!
Ruby looked, across the freaking street
Saw Pam, standing, on her two big feet;
Ruby yelled, you need to leave this block
Before I clean, your dog-gone clock.
Birdman yelled, get her Pam, get her good
whip her ass, all over, this neighborhood;
Pam stepped across the street
Forearmed Ruby Red, off her feet.
Stomped Ruby, upside the head
Up walked Ruby's husband, Freaky Fred;
Fred said, I'm here to get my wife
Birdman yelled, you better take, some good advice,
Leave this place, right away
Before we make you have to stay;

Birdman began, to laugh and chirp
Fred sprung on him like Wyatt Earp.
A left to the jaw, and a right to his neck
Left Birdman looking, like an Andretti wreck;
Before Fred, could turn around
Pam Pistol whipped him to the ground.
By then, Ruby had gained her composure
Blindsided Pam, like a bull dozier;
Ruby grabbed Fred, jumped into the Cadillac
Sped off Yelling, dammit, we'll be back!
Before they made, two city blocks
That Caddy slammed, into two rogue cops;
Where you two, speeding, off to so fast?
From them two, coming to kick our ass.
Up popped Pam, in that big dam hummer
On the case, like a stealth bomber
Those Dogs fought, through the night
Before the National Guard, broke up that fight.
The next dam day, the newspapers read Arrested,
Pam, Birdman, Ruby, and Freaky Fred
And we hope, this God-Dam brawl is finally dead!

"UNCLE PETE"

Down in Soulsville, lived a man named Pete
The toughest Scutter, on the street;
The corner of King and Ford, was his spot
Gambling and pretty women, made it hot.

From Friday evening, to late Sunday night
Crap games are pumping, money is tight;
Pete was the house-man, and ran things straight
But plenty of gangstas, just loved to hate.
Up and down, is the Hustler life
Dreams someday, of having a wife;
Once again, stuff hits the fan
Pete must play, the gangsta hand.
This wanna be, Queen Late-fa witch
Grabbed Pete, by his freaking wrist;
Pete yelled, woman, what's your trouble
Mess around, and I'll bust your bubble.
She replied,
You have no respect for a lady, that's a fact
Pete answered, first, you gotta get up, off your
back.
What you mean? I dance in rap videos
That maybe reason, some look at you, like whores.

Pete, that's hard work, and good money
if you were not stupid, you would be funny.
Listen up, I ain't no dam hick
why you out there twerk'in, and turning tricks
This is how I get paper, by shaking my ass
Now, you're Donald Trump, and want a pass?
That tells me, you don't have any class.
You selling yourself for now and later
That's a fact, and I ain't no hater;
So, if you shaking ass in videos,
And getting down on all fours,
The world calls it modern whores.
///

"MINNY MIKE SCHOOLS JIMMY YACK"

Way down South, in the bottom land
Lives an old, angry ass, shitty man;
Never had much, and never will
Only promotes, a messed-up deal.

He blames the world, for his fate
He Loves to lie, and loves to hate;
Who but a fool, despise their life
Who but a fool, prefers much strife;
With all due respect, this is fact
The idiot's name, is Jimmy Yack.
Jimmy Yack, is a turd, of the first order
Don't let this buzzard, near your daughter;
He eats raw skunk, and drinks possum piss
This misfit comes from, deep in the abyss.
Watch this geek, when he comes around
He takes everything, not nailed down;
He will even hide, in a deep dark pit
He will give Dolomite, a dog-gone fit.
Then sit down, and eat a bowl of grit
And say, it's just, another, freaking bit;
But, I'm about, to make him split
Because, Minny Mike don't ever quit.
Like a diet, I trim trouble, in many ways
But You don't lose this trouble, in 21 days;

I slide over things, like a Jamaican bobsled
Keep messing around, and you wake up dead.
Yes, my tongue is hard, like a night stick
I bust brains, with this Mack-Neat-O-Kit;
I hate quail, and I'm partial to duck
Look in the dictionary, I am bad luck.
I quash problems with these rhymes
Guess what, its daylight-saving times;
Jimmy Yack thinks, it's a childish game
I'm gonna give him, his hour of fame.
I peel back, a loser's cap
Try to stand-up, to all this rap;
Call a doctor, if you must
Better yet, The Mid-Atlantic Trust;
Nevertheless, from dawn to dusk
I'm on the case, until your heart bust.
And never-mind, your baby feelings

Like a card-shark, watch my dealings;
If you must know, the winner's rule
Get ready to go, back to school.
I ain't your momma, nor your daddy
Like Tiger Woods, you my Caddy;
Yardage me wrong, suffer the fate
Think of my wrath, as a blind date.
Rhyming ain't dead, understand this Mit
Some lazy poets, just wanna quit;
Those are the rules, they don't lie
These rhymes are law, until the pigs fly.

"FRANK VS JOHNNY LUMP LUMP"

Fourth of July, back in '94
A heavy knock, on Frank's door;
Who the Huck, could this be
It better be, something free.
Frank opens the door, to his surprise
Johnny Lump Lump, in his eyes;
What the Huck, an indecent exposure
I thought this beef, was to a closure.
This is what, Johnny Lump Lump said
I ain't forgot Frank, you bust my head;
Frank replied, you lucky you ain't dead
And another thing, don't be misled.
This rhyming is still, alive and well
Get it twisted, and I'll ring your bell;
I'll lump up your face, like I did before
If you don't leave, my damned door!
Frank, your threats mean, diddly to me
I'm Johnny Lump Lump, from Tennessee;
I'm gonna scan your ass, like McAfee
Clean you up, and set you free;
Then delete, your musty memory.

I'm Johnny Lump Lump, I don't play
I leave a pigga, with nothing to say;
I'm on my job, every night and day
Like the Grimm Reaper, I make you pray.
Johnny Lump Lump, shut the Huck up
Before you angry me up, like the Hulk;
I'm FrakeinFace, from Jaybow's House
Hacking up impostors, with this mouth.
Since I was a baby, I been talking shit
Straight from the womb, and never quit;
I swam across the Atlantic, to get to the other side
I swam back, because, I wasn't freaking tired.
I fought a polar bear, with a tooth pick
Made that big monster, turn and quit;
I ran a cheetah down, on the African plain
The Big Cat said, you're a bad ass mane.
I wrestled an elephant, they called it a wreck
The rhinos bowed down, and gave me respect;
The hucking lions got jealous, started to growl
I ruffed them up so bad, the Game Warden, called
it fowl.
So, Johnny Lump Lump, you got 3 seconds to leave
Before I have fire squirting, from your draws and
sleeves;

Johnny Lump Lump tried, to make his pleas'
Frank knocked him, to his freaking knees.
It's been 22 years, since that vicious scene
To be exact its now, Twenty Sixteen (2016);
There's been several sightings, of Johnny, since
that day
But he has never been sighted, around
Frank's way.
FrankenFace Forest

"LILLY LASS"

This is my story, I'm Lilly Lass
A mean woman, of the first class;
I make your man ask, when he scream
How a woman so fine, can be so mean?

I'll love your man, and tell you why
He needs a good woman, that's no lie;
I'm not about, a lotta bull and talk
My secret weapon, is the slut walk.
If your butt don't wobble, & poke, out
You ain't got no real, freaking clout;
I know exactly, what your man need
A good ass, chance, to plant his seed.
Like Lou Reed, call me Sweet Jane
Some good advice, stay in your lane;
I handle my game, without any fear
Like Sharon Stone, on Richard Gere.
I'm a poetic woman, night and day
I ain't got no time,. for childish play;
If you don't believe, just ask Barack
I'm Like Michelle, I stay on the clock.
For the record again, I'm Lilly Lass
With a big black, sweet, piece of class;
I shake this BO-Dunk-A-Dunk, real fast
It want break, 'cause it ain't no glass';

Like Layla Ali, I don't take no sass
Like Donald Trump, I want my pass;
With Gregory Hines and his class
I'll tap dance on, a bitch's ass.
and order a plate, of baked bass
Wash it down, with a gallon of gas
Then blow a fireball, on that ass
Finally, call a Priest, to hold mass.
If the beef must go, to round two
This is what the Huck, happens to you;
You will hear a loud, coo coo clock
When I seed that butt, with a glock.
If that don't decide, your future fate
I'll throw, this combo like a .38;
And if you still, talking your jive
I'm gonna hit you up, like a .45,
And if you make it, to the freaking door
I'm sending you out, with a left foot .44
I'm the number 1 shot caller, in my class
All you heifers, remember, I'm Lilly Lass!

"SUPER MOUTH MEETS DANNY DOG"

This is a hucked-up story, I must tell
About this cancer, straight from hell;
A mean-mother, with no empathy
But always want, your sympathy.
It was a foggy, fall day, in Capitol Heights
One of those days, that's, just not right;
The cat don't meow, the dog don't bark
When the day turns, to gangsta dark.
I was riding the strip, making my round
Sheriff and Division, the NE side of town;
And up pops this big, black, shiny hog
Behind the wheel, sits Danny Dog.
Now, Dog been ducking me for days
Because he got some doggy dog ways;
I boxed him in, and told him to sit still
I said, better yet, pay your freaking bill.
Dog responded,
Huck you Super, and your rhyming crew

I'm Danny Dog, I'm known to spit too;
I rob minds, and make' em cry
Keep hucking with me, you gonna die.
Dog, I ain't your sucker, I tell you no more
Your ass is mine, when you exit, that door;
Dog jumped out, and reached for his gat
I sprung on his butt, with a rata tata tat tat;
Dog screamed, Super do you hear?
The cops are coming, they awfully near
Super, hit Dog, and Rhymes flew out his ear.
By then, a cop pulled up, in a Crown
Super laid, that poetic rhyming down.
Danny Dog reached, for his gat again
Two more D.C. cops, rounded the bend;
That's when Super, got in the wind
Left that block, with a big ass grin;
Sipping on julep, rum, and gin;
yelling, Catch me Big Dog, if you can.
Cops shouted out a word at his ass
But Super was just, too dam fast;
Danny Dog, peeled off, the other way With a chance,
to fight, another day.

"NAY NAY NOOKY"

Nay Nay Nooky, is her name
The meanest thang, in the game
At the age of 18, she owned, 24 sports cars
By 21, she owned, a string of gambling bars.
On a cold, blistery, Winter, Memphis night
Pooky Slim, started a serious, freaking fight;
He broke, Two Jaw Jake's, bad left leg
Comatosed Nay Nay's, Uncle Greg;
Jumped over the bar, and busted a keg
And these are, the exact words, he said:
If you ain't with me, you better go
Because Nay Nay, don't run, this no-more
Matter of fact, I'm running this dam show.
Nay Nay stepped out, the back-room door
With a blade, some knucks, and a PH .44;
Wearing a micro mini, and nylon skinnies
Looking like a babe, out the roaring 20's.
Pooky looked at Nooky, and said, God-Dam
I'm gonna get me, a piece of that juicy ham;

Slid over the bar, grabbed his cell phone
Took a selfie, said baby, let's get it on.
Nay Nay slugged Pooky, with them knucks
He started doing, the huck-a-buck;
Hit the jukebox, and it came on
Blasting JB's, "Only in America Song."
Nay Nay hit Pooky's head, with that blade
Gave that sucker, a finial fade
Pooky straighten up, and ran for the door
Nay Nay bust him, in the ass, with that .44
Stood over him, and ask, want some more?
Because I can reload, and let this baby go!
The crowd let out, a deep, freaking moan
And begged Nay Nay, to leave Pooky alone;
Nay Nay said, this .44 has done me proud
Then parted the crowd and spoke out loud.
Remember, My Name, is Nay Nay Nooky
I ain't no meow type, of cutely pussy
I slap tricks around, with this cookie
And I dam sure ain't no, freaking Rooky;
Huck with me, and I'll lay your ass down
Because, I run, this dog-gone town.

"WHITNEY HOUSTON"
(THE DAY OUR INNOCENCE DIED)

"Whitney Houston"
(The Day Our Innocence Died)

We will never forget,
The rains came, the skies turned grey
It seemed to rain, on the world that day;
And all creation, became hopelessly sad
The pain we suffered, for the loss we had;
Knowing that she, would never be again
The world has lost, a real dear friend.

And the wind, blew silent,
And all the animals, pranced, and moaned
While earth, stood still, and sadly groaned
For that, was the day, the universe cried
That was the day, Whitney Houston died......

She was the apple, of a young man's eye
She was the virtue, girls, could admire

Never once giving in, to an earthly lust
Always singing, the one, we could trust
We took for granted, she would be around
She lifted our spirits, with her every sound
And now, we all hold, our heads down.

And the wind, blew silent,
And all the animals, pranced, and moaned
While earth, stood still, and sadly groaned
For that, was the day, the universe cried
That was the day, Whitney Houston died......

No more days, of old cuisine
No more looks, in magazines;
Every boy, and every girl
Cry for her, in this ole world;
no tear, can replace her love
She flew away, like a dove.

And the wind, blew silent,
And all the animals, pranced, and moaned

While earth, stood still, and sadly groaned
For that, was the day, the universe cried
That was the day, Whitney Houston died......

From shore, to shore, we all weep
This sad secret, we could not keep
We all felt the pain, tragically deep;
When the world looses, a real true friend
It's so very hard, to start over again.
The truth is, it could never, ever be
For we're human, and could not see
Until it truly happened, to you and me.

And the wind, blew silent,
And all the animals, pranced, and moaned
While earth, stood still, and sadly groaned
For that, was the day, the universe cried
That was the day, Whitney Houston died......

ABOUT THE BOOK... "FEELINGS 2022"

FEELINGS 2022 IS AN EXTENTION OF WOODROW WALLACE'S MORDERN DAY POETRY. FEELINGS OPENS WITH THE CURRENT EVENTS OF 2022 AND EXPOSES DEEP EMOTIONAL REACTIONS STEMMING FROM THE TIMES OF COVID 19... WHICH HAS KILLED MILLIONS OF PEOPLE.

ACTORS AROUND THE WORLD, SUCH AS RUSSIA, CHINA, IRAN, AND A FEW OTHERS DEPENDENT ON RUSSIA'S FUEL LIKE INDIA ARE PRESENTLY MOVING TOWARD COMPLETELY CHANGING THE WAY WESTERN COUNTRIES OPERATE GLOBALLY.

THIS BOOK ALSO SHOWCASES THE SENSATIONAL STORY TELLING BY THE AUTHOR, WHO ENTERTAINS THE

READER WHILE FOCUSING ON A VARIETY OF MORDERN URBAN
POETRY PIECES. WOODROW WALLACE EVOKES LAUGHTER
AND SADNESS WHILE ARTICULATING A CHILD LIKE MANISH ADVENTURE IN TIMES OF EPIDEMIC UPHEAVAL WITH "FEELINGS 2022".

"DISREGUARD YOUR PAST &
FORFIET YOUR FUTURE"
-WOODROW WALLACE

ABOUT THE AUTHOR.....

WOODROW WALLACE IS A NATIVE OF MEMPHIS, TENNESSEE WHERE HE WAS FORMALLY EDUCATED. THE AUTHOR IS A GRADUTE OF THE UNIVERSITY OF PHOENIX WITH A DEGREE IN BUSINESS MANAGEMENT AND IS KNOWN FOR HIS WORKS OF MODERN DAY POETRY AND PHYLOSPHY.

THE AUTHOR WILL ENTRIQUE THE READER WITH HIS
ABILITIES TO STIMULATE THE IMAGINATION AND FULFILL AN EXCITING ADVENTURE WITH POETRY. WOODROW WALLACE
IS TRULY A MODERN DAY POET.

Printed in the United States
by Baker & Taylor Publisher Services